"Quick, effective motivational & marketing messages driving you to success"

Intention Trumps Time

Vol. 17 In The *Sub 4 Minute Extra Mile* Series

by

Dr. Ted Ciuba

Intention Trumps Time

Vol. 17 In The *Sub 4 Minute Extra Mile* Series

ISBN: 978-1477578407

by **Ted Ciuba**

www.ThinkRich.com
info@holomagic.com
Parthenon Marketing Inc
2400 Crestmoor Rd #36
Nashville TN 37215   USA

Orders & Enrollments
+1-877- *4 RICHES*
***
phone +1-615-662-3169
fax: +1-615-369-9749

 Contact Ted Ciuba about speaking for or training your group or organization.

Ted Ciuba is also the author of the incredible modernization and empowerment of Napoleon Hill's success classic, *Think & Grow Rich!*

Ted Ciuba
The New Think & Grow Rich
Author of Sub 4 Minute Extra Mile Series
Author of *The New Think And Grow Rich*

"This is **more than just a revamp with modern examples** - it radically transforms the vision by adding new gender, cross-cultural and international issues to the mix, including new material to include both science and genetics, as in the Quantum reality of accelerating income and wealth.

An excellent re-do of a classic financial inspirational guide."

Tamara Doris

"The writing is so much more applicable and understandable that I am literally forcing my friends, colleagues, and mastermind members to get their copies now!

Every page fills me with passion and revs me up!"

T.J. Rohleder

"I picked up Ted's book -- AND I WAS SHOCKED AND AMAZED! I sat there and began going through it ... and all of a sudden looked up and over 3 hours had gone by!!! I quickly read it from cover to cover within 2 days and then turned around and did it again! Ted has done a truly amazing thing, by totally re-writing this powerful classic. Every entrepreneur and business owner simply MUST have Ted's book!"

"You Are Closer To A Million Dollar$ Than You Now Dream!"

This is the modernized, quantum empowered version of Napoleon Hill's success classic , *Think And Grow Rich!*

#1 Best-Seller

An instruction manual to *consciously* direct the Quantum universe to manifest your positive desires."

Napoleon Hill Overlooks Ted Ciuba
Physical, Kindle. iStore

Are you ready for breakthrough progress overnight?!

Engage with *The New Think And Grow Rich* - empower yourself! Start exactly where you are - no experience, no education, no cash required! Discover how to…

- Trigger the *self-fulfilling prophecy* and the *law of attraction*!
- Apply the insights of the secret "combination" to work for your immediate, easy success
- Direct the Quantum universe to deliver success
- Unleash that powerful "HoloMagic c2 factor" to accomplish your pursuits in a fraction of the time, with only a quanta of the effort to reap HUGE, AMAZING, WINDFALL results!

Mark Whyborn, UK

*"I have read **The New Think And Grow Rich** and there is a **HUGE** improvement (so much more insight) in the new updated version!*

Once you learn the formula to riches, you can apply it to accelerate your income into the stratosphere!

Order now, for you and your company & loved ones. Available at http://www.amazon.com, www.BarnesAndNoble.com, & any reputable bookstore.

www.ThinkRich.com/book

TABLE OF CONTENTS

CONTENTS

Vol. 17 In *The Sub 4 Minute Extra Mile* Series

INTENTION TRUMPS TIME

by

Dr. Ted Ciuba

Introduction: It Takes So Little To Excel

As an achiever, would you agree with me that you must go the extra mile? *I thought so...*

Surely you know if you do what average people do, you'll get the same kind of average results they do. And something tells me you're a cut above that!

And it's actually quite easy to stand out, because most people wouldn't dream of going the extra mile. But for you and me, while, yes, it takes something extra, yes, it takes drive and discipline…. The amazing thing is, it takes so *little* to excel!

Roger Bannister
Runs Sub 4 Minute Mile

After all, it's called the extra *mile*, not the extra *100 miles!*

Be that as it may, we're talking about the positive rewards that come to you in any economy by going the extra mile.

It was Roger Bannister who defied and redefined history by running the sub 4 minute mile.

And the amazing thing is that Bannister did NOT spend the countless hours and hours practicing that conventional training would guide him to. He gave it what he could... In his busy pre-med Oxford schedule he took a mere 30 minutes out of his daily lunch hour to train and run. And with that he set a world record that had towered 3,000 years!

He ushered in a new era of possibility. Though no one had *ever* broken it, within 2 1/2 years time of Bannister's record-breaking, seemingly unachievable sub 4 minute mile, 18 others were doing it.

And how did he do it?... It wasn't a function of *time*. Conventional sports training encompasses hours on an almost daily basis, not 30 minutes!!

It was *intention*. Roger Bannister, in the short, focused, regular, intense, intended few minutes per day he wrested from his busy Oxford pre-med studies was throwing himself into the sport. He gave it everything he could, as an additional interest and pursuit in his life...

You see, when Roger Bannister suffered the ignominious defeat of coming in 5th place in the 1952 Olympics, right then and there, he determined to be the first human to run the sub 4 minute mile!

It was just a "thought". It's just another instance and undisputable illustration, my friend, of the power of intention powered by determination.

Moments before 6 pm on 6 May 1954, he takes a breath of vision and determination. He feels it! He confides to his pacemakers "The sub 4 minute attempt is on!"

Short moments later the shot is fired... The runners are off!! Roger Bannister breaks the string at the end of the mile in 3 minutes, 59 seconds, and 4/10's, trailblazing into the sub 4 minute mile age!

Recognition Point!! - This was NOT an unintended event! Recognition point!! Little efforts, little accomplishments - short, focused, regular, intense, intended training sessions - gear into colossal events!

Also note how little it takes to stand waaay beyond the competition! Roger Bannister redefined history in one evening... And he did it only with the razor's edge of difference, 1/10 of a second over 1/2 of a second!!!

This didn't happen by circumstance... Roger Bannister didn't "drift" over the finish line into the annals of history... It was the thing he geared all his intentions to accomplish, even though he didn't spend hours and hours a day in the quest to achieve it.

Which gives rise to the name of this series, The *Sub 4 Minute Extra Mile* Series...

Now you, honoring Roger Bannister's history-setting accomplishments and methods, can make the same kind of history-breaking progress in sub 4 minutes a day! Defy the status quo in short, focused, regular, intense, intended training sessions and redefine what's possible and what you accomplish!

ENTHUSIASM IS NOT "SOME" THING IT'S EVERYTHING!

Featuring Glenn W. Turner

I was broadcasting in the company of several legendary marketers... Really, a dream come true...

And it came my turn to comment on "enthusiasm". And while I have much to say on the topic and your weal-being, HoloMagic in the moment had gifted us with the company of a very special achiever, so I deferred to the legendary Glenn W. Turner.

This is a man who, just in case you don't know, built an international business conglomerate of 78 corporations in 27 countries, generating over $100 Million in 3 years... There's also over 1,000 millionaires who personally swear their fortunes to their association with Glenn W. Turner.

Glenn confidently and honorably accepted the mic, thanked me graciously, and began...

> Let me talk about enthusiasm in my life. You're listening to a guy born in a charity ward from an unwed mother in 1934, who's 75 years young. And I had nothing going for me. I had no money, I had no prestige, I had no important friends. A fella that made $10,000 a year was a special person to me.

> So all I had to start with was enthusiasm, and I got excited. I got excited about a chance that I might become a multi-millionaire, and I might be happy 24 hours a day, in spite of me talking through my nose, and having an 8th grade education. I simply went out and set myself on fire, and everybody got burned in the flame I put out.

> So enthusiasm is *everything*. It's not "some" thing, it's EVERYTHING. It's the God within you. I have always been excited, because when you're around someone, do you want to be around somebody dragging their feet or looking down their nose—or do you want to have somebody with enthusiasm inside them?

> Excited people are enthusiastic people, and it's as simple and plain as that. If you get enthusiasm you get money, if you get enthusiasm you get happiness, if you get enthusiasm you get a lot of friends. So enthusiasm is what it's all about.

NOTES

Item / passage / page	Insight	Action

WHAT BUSINESS ARE YOU REALLY IN?

Featuring Michael Penland

Recently top marketer Michael Penland and myself were leading a small group, talking about the secrets of succeeding in our field, and here's one of the things Michael shared:

> Understanding what business you're really in can double, triple, or even quadruple your income. So I want to begin by asking you a question—it's the same question I ask at every seminar I ever conduct, and of every business owner with whom I do consulting. I want to ask you this question right now.
>
> The question is this: 'What business are you in?'
>
> You know, 99 out of 100 people who are asked that question will give the wrong answer. See, most of them will tell me their business is either marketing, or real estate, or network marketing, or health products, or information products, or chiropractor, or carpet cleaner, or this, or that, or whatever—some other business.
>
> You know, here's the bottom line... All of us are really in the same business. There's just one business, and we're all in it, or we *should* be, and the business we're in is the people business, the relationship business.
>
> Now let me say that again, guys. You're in the relationship business. If you're not, you're really not in business at all. You're really not.
>
> I want to share with you the magic formula that's earned me a fortune as a marketer. I call this formula the CTRC Formula. That's an acronym—I love acronyms.
>
> The *C* in that formula stands for *credibility*. That's the quality, or the capacity, or the capability, to get someone to believe you.
>
> Now, I've got a question for you: do you believe everybody and everything they tell you? Well, of course not.
>
> The *T* stands for *trust*. Again, do you trust everybody? Well, no. Well, listen up, my friend, I've got some news for you. If that's true of you, it's also true of those people to whom you're marketing, to whom you're selling.

Surf www.ThinkRich.com * Quantum Business Acceleration, $197 value gift *FREE*

Very few people out there in the marketplace you're selling to or marketing to feel like they can really rely upon your integrity, your abilities, your character. Quite simply, they don't trust you.

And the *R* in that formula stands for *relationship*. Again, I ask you, "What business are you in?"

Understand the people who whom you're marketing have no relationship with you. You must establish a good relationship to earn their business. And today's consumers, amongst today's competitive options, are more demanding than ever.

And the *C* in that formula stands for *cash*... And that's what everyone wants, isn't it? That's what you want, isn't it?

If you were happy with your thing, if you'd made all the money you already wanted to make, you wouldn't be reading this, would you? But the reason you're here is because you've got what it takes to be successful. And this CTRC formula can help you reach new levels of achievement.

You see, sadly, most marketers—most people—believe that if they get enough cash, they can have a relationship, they can have trust, and they can have credibility with other people. They get the formula reversed, and it simply doesn't work that way. I've been doing this 40 years. It just doesn't work in reverse.

So, what do you do as a marketer, as a salesperson? Well, through systematic marketing what you try to do is to attract the largest number of people who are the most qualified to buy what you're selling. And then you try to prove to them that you have what they want, that you're trustworthy, and that you're gonna fulfill on all of your promises.

And you do that by making them feel that you really care about them, not just a little, but a lot. That you've got their best interests at heart. And then you continue to do the things that make them know you're really their friend.

Now, you know I know that sounds simple, and you know, it really is. But don't let the simplistic nature of what I'm sharing with you here keep you from understanding the real power of building a relationship business.

IF I HAD LISTENED TO THE PEOPLE BACK HOME...
Featuring Glenn W. Turner

Today, folks, I want to share some more of the inspiring words of my friend, marketing legend Glenn W. Turner!!...

The first thing to remember is that you have to go to seminars. What changed my life was *not* listening to my neighbors and my friends, my father, my mother, and the people in my small town. If I'd listened to them, I'd have been pumping gas at a gas station, driving a taxi cab, or just working some average job.

And there's nothing wrong being average, if you're happy. But very few people are.

What you have to do is go to seminars. I have spent, over my lifetime, hundreds of thousands of dollars going to seminars, even though I've taken in $300 million selling my own seminar, and I've done it in five languages.

Because at seminars you are with people of like minds—you're not around your neighbors and your friends and people who put you down, you're around people who are there for the same reason you are, to learn from the best.

And Michael Penland, Ted Ciuba, and Dale Calvert are three of the best I've ever seen. And I'm just proud to be associated with 'em, and the fact that they let an old man like me come around and say a few words, and still keep me alive.

Think about it, I'm 75 years young. How else can a hare-lipped, 8th grade drop-out, born in a charity ward from an unwed mother, go into 27 countries around the world, own 20 airplanes, four of 'em jets, and build 78 corporations if I didn't learn from someone *other* than the people I grew up with?

So if you're not happy, if you're not successful, if you're not doubling or tripling your income, then you're simply listening to and associating with the wrong people. Sometimes it's your wife—she needs a seminar better than you do, so she doesn't drag you down. Sometimes it's your husband, and they need a seminar.

Surf www.ThinkRich.com * Quantum Business Acceleration, $197 value gift *FREE*

Sometimes it's just anybody—your friends, so-called friends. So you've got to go to seminars just like you go to a revival in a church, like in the old days...I've learned that. Revivals revive you, where you can double, and triple, and even quadruple your income, or even do better than that.

I have built over 1,000 millionaires. They're in the trucking business, they're in the gas station business. Travel America—some of my boys own that. They net $4 million a year with four truck stops. I've got real estate people, I've got doctors, lawyers, politicians— they all went to seminars.

The people that attend the most seminars and read the most positive books like *Think and Grow Rich*, which turned my life around, that Ted's got in *The NEW Think And Grow Rich*, those are the people that succeed in this life.

So in finishing up on this subject, if you want to double, triple, or even quadruple your income, or even better than that, you have got to go and associate with people who are doing it, not talking it.

YOU ARE IN THE RELATIONSHIP BUSINESS

There are certain things that are just so obvious that we don't even see them. Like, for example, the way a fish doesn't know that it's in water. And like this statement: "Honesty is the best policy."

You know, the people who taught me that "honesty is the best policy" were teaching me from a moral/religious point of view, and I'm grateful for it. But it never occurred to them that really is true in all things.

If you're not running an honest ship, you're destroying yourself. That's the way the world works; that's the way nature works. So honesty really is the best policy, even if you take religion and morality out of it.

The same thing's true about any business you're in. It *is* a relationship business. Look: only thieves, terrorists, and governments use guns to take what they want. The rest of us have to make sales. To use persuasion. To make money, it's going to take working with people so you get repeat and upgrade sales. You give more service to the people you've got, and that's all. It's *all* about relationships.

What if you're a banker? Aren't all banks more or less equal? What if you're in the gas station business—aren't all gas stations more or less equal? Now, if you get a clerk in one of those places who gives you a problem, it's real easy for you to say, "Well, I'm never going back."

And it might be that you change your banks, or just go to a different branch, depending on your situation. But that's a clear example of how everybody has seen a relationship sour.

On the other hand, you naturally prefer to tend to and favor the businesses who make you feel like they appreciate you. That's natural.

A lot of times we don't see obvious things. We're *in* the relationship business, and that is the *only* business we're in. Everything else is the way we do things or the things we do it with. We've got strategic systems, we've got our product, we've got expertise— but it's a people business.

NOTES

Item / passage / page	Insight	Action

AND THEN WE HAVE A CHRISTMAS TREE

I'm not any different than you—people want instant results. Sometimes people ask me about the coaching program I offer. The most popular is a 12-week program in which we get together once a week for 50 minutes, and I coach people on business building, life enhancement, and getting their head straight around their projects.

That's most important on a group level – as in we offer this product as a MasterMind, in which many people come together, and also as a specialized, company / project specific level.

We always follow the principles of *The NEW Think and Grow Rich*. Research, organized planning, study, develop a plan, get into *action*.

Even those few people who even know what they want, seldom get into action.

So we do this and they ask, "Why can't you just do like so-and-so did, and bring us all into a seminar and instead of charging us $3,000, charge us $2,000 and everything's good and quick?"

Well, believe me, I'm just like you, I know that would be preferable—and that is exactly what I would do if it really worked.

The problem is the kind of deep, committed, personal change, with checks and balances, is a new lifestyle, because, essentially, it's what you do with your time that is going to determine your *results*. And there are so many things—from *fear* and lack of self-confidence, to lack of knowing, to not having resources—that can get in your way.

Hey, just think about it like this—it's like the Christmas tree. You know, I would like to say a few hocus-pocus words, abracadabra, shazam, and *bam*! Christmas tree's up, lookin' good, presents are underneath it... but it doesn't work that way, does it?

We begin with the journey to the lot on a cold, crisp, day if we're in certain parts of the world... in other certain parts it could be a very warm day. We bring it home, and that's even an adventure. And we have to bring it home cleanly so that we don't have to clean up behind us.

We have to get it up—that could be an adventure. I've been the Daddy all my life, when I wasn't the son, right? But I learned from my Daddy, so I know what Daddy is doing, too. Daddy has to put the lights on.

And then, of course, there's somebody cooking something, and the aroma's in the house, and there's Christmas music on, and the family is playing—we are having an *experience*.

And once Daddy gets the lights on, of course Mamma is going to be the one who gives the final visual check and approval. Daddy can adjust, and then everybody gathers around and we orderly—well, semi-orderly, we put on all the other decorations and the final things like icicles, and we make sure the sheet underneath is orderly.

And then we start bringing in the presents, and *that* actually is an adventure in its own self which continues right up to the moment the final guest or family member arrives before our particular family's hour of celebration….

And *then* we have a Christmas tree. *Beautiful*, total, complete, ready to do the miles.

And now you know why we have, and recommend, and deliver to you a 12-week coaching / consulting program over a single pop, *fast, flash.*

WHATEVER THE THEMES OF TODAY ARE TODAY IS THE TIME TO EMBRACE THEM

I've been a writer since the age of seven years old. No kidding, I did start turning out product until the age of 20-21—though I knew at seven that that's what I wanted to be. I was struck with destiny during an ordinary moment. I've had this passion for 50 years. I'm 57 now as I write this moment.

And so I've basically always had this passion, this knowledge that, whatever it is you're going to do, whatever it is you want to feel, experience, express, or explain—again, I'm coming at it as a writer—*you gotta do it now*.

Because *now* you have the energy, *now* you have the feeling. Guaranteed—I've lived through this thing in generation after generation, decade after decade, because later you won't have the same feeling. Not the same way. Not with the same animation.

For instance, here's one *little* thing. I just met a guy who's 18 years old and he's talking about how he's going to go out with his girlfriend tonight. Well, now, I still go out with my girlfriend. And I'm still getting excited, but it's not the *most* important thing in the entire world that could ever happen, like it was when I was 18, right?

Times have passed...we don't get a chance to repeat. Whatever the themes of today are, today *is* the time to embrace them.

Hey, there are so many things where everybody says, "Well, if I had known when I was 21 what I know now, I would have done things differently…. Well, if I only had the chance to do it all over again…"

And what's that old German saying, "Too quick old, too late smart?"

Easy to say… Just get this: we don't get a chance to repeat.

Whatever the themes of today are today *is* the time to embrace them.

NOTES

Item / passage / page	Insight	Action

TAKE ADVANTAGE OF THE BENEFITS THIS TIME DOES BRING

There's a person who does some work for me—getting specific, she does transcriptions for me—who off and on has done it for years. We've been creating product all this time... Of course, most of it earlier was Internet-related, and she came right along with that.

And now, most of what I do is actually oriented around *The NEW Think and Grow Rich* and empowerment technologies, such as the article that you're reading right now.

Who do you think made the transcript? It's her. First off—no, don't ask me for her name if you're an information marketer, because she's doing a *good job*. And my advice is, find your own, dude or dudetta!

But here is the truth—I have used her for years off and on. And I've been using her intensely during this economic recession, because hey, man, *we're* not slowing down.

The economy may have, over all, entered into a period of turmoil and morass, and my investments, the buy and hold ones, those have softened dramatically. A lot of things have changed and you know that, but our business—we're not slowing down, no way. We're honkin'... People need us more than ever. We're creating more than ever.

And when paid work slows down, that's a good time to do more of the creative work that was hard to get to when business was growing so dramatically.

And so I sent some stuff off to her recently, a good chunk, with the message, "Thanks for being so special, I really appreciate what you do," and that is the truth: I really do, I really have. Hey, she is good, she is specific, we are in flow together, things are working well. I really appreciate it...I've got to have someone do it.

And she writes back, "No, thank *you* for being the answer to a prayer."

You see, her business actually *has* slowed down. A lot of information marketers—and to be precise, that is the field that I happen to be in, one of the people who create audios, videos, books, e-books, this kind of stuff—have backed off.

For all of the above reasons, most people aren't taking advantage of the benefits this time does bring.

She can take anything, whether it's a television program or a teleconference we've recorded, or just a dictation into a mike, and turn it into a typed transcript.

Her business has slowed down, and she was concerned, and she was praying. About that time we send her a whole new project to pick up the slack – for our own needs, not hers... But it was the answer to a prayer to her. That's *HoloMagic*!

All I can say is, hey, it's like the famous song or prayer Francis of Assisi is credited with writing: "Make Me An Instrument Of Your Peace". I love that song. And I love being, for you and for all the world, for all the history, for all the time that comes, with due respect to my helpers who make it possible. Don't you just love being an emissary for HoloMagic.

FLYING BACKWARDS IN TIME

I will never forget one particular trip. I've had a lot of trip adventures—I love to travel. Like the time I came back from China. I left early in the morning from China, and I arrived on the same day, in Nashville, Tennessee.

Now, you can do that because of the time zone difference, and it's a long trip and you're flying backwards in time, and all these kind of things. But it was interesting when I walked into my favorite Chinese restaurant and said, "Yeah, yeah, oh, I was in China this morning."

"No! No way!"

"Yes, I was. You can see it, look here, here's some money." I gave 'em some Chinese currency. We're always changing money back and forth, because they're always traveling to China also, and we're both money collectors, et cetera—but that's a whole 'nother story.

That's an interesting travel story. Now here's another one—time travel. Look, folks, I don't know if this has happened to you yet or not, but let me share the experience with you. I live currently in la Ciudad de Panamá, Panamá and Nashville, Tennessee.

I *have* lived in a number of other cities in the U.S., including the Dallas/Ft. Worth area, the Los Angeles/San Diego areas, my favorites, and Denver. But I go away, I go into Los Angeles, San Diego, Fresno, Sacramento, and I come *back* to Nashville some eight or nine years later.

The traveling to California was a *real* cool epoch. That's where I got my certification in hypnosis, that's where I studied profoundly—the study and experience were more profound, obviously, than that certification. That's where I fire-walked thousands of times, that's where I taught and led hundreds and hundreds at a time to fire-walk.

*That'*s where I came into my spiritual maturity. That's where Yoga, that's where Sri Krishna, that's where Eckankar, that's where the Rosicrucians, that's where dozens and dozens of other things became optimal influences in my life, not the least of which was Ernest Holmes.

But coming back was a shock. I want you to know, what I did was, I went to one of the new thought churches—it was named Unity in Nashville. You can still go there, it's called First Church Unity.

I just sauntered back in...*I* hadn't changed any during the last eight or nine years since I had seen them. At least I didn't *know* that I had, I didn't feel that I had, didn't see that I had. It never even occurred to me.

Within *five minutes* of being inside that church with those people I knew, all kinds of changes became obvious. It was so shocking that within five minutes I'm *screaming* to the men's room, and I'm looking at myself in front of that big mirror that takes up the entire wall.

I want to see if *I* have changed as dramatically as they have. If *my* hair has gone gray, if my posture has changed, if *my* belly, my waistline has exploded, if my hair has thinned away. I'm just like, "What's going on?" Finally I looked and I concluded, "Not me!"

DO IT DELIBERATELY, WITH PASSION AND INTENT

If you are bilingual, I highly recommend that you pick up your own copy of *El Nuevo Piense y Hágase Rico*, because I believe you will find a lot of help here. Sometimes it's just when the light reflects on it in a different way that you see something different and more profound.

I can assure you that having read *Think and Grow Rich*, the original by Napoleon Hill, over 77 times, when I was charged with the responsibility to write *The NEW Think and Grow Rich*—oh, I began re-reading it again, and I began thinking deeply and more profoundly.

And I also traveled to Columbia—Cali, Columbia to be exact, and it was the mall at Chipe Chape, at The Man From La Mancha bookstore, where I picked up my copy of the original *Piense y Hágase Rico*. And I read the entire book for the new insights.

Just like I said, sometimes it's just the glint of light, or the reflection is different so that it penetrates deeper, or it hits your eyeballs the right way—you know what I mean, and it was effective.

Likewise, reading *The NEW Think and Grow Rich* in Spanish – my own book, translated by someone more capable than me, is doing the same thing for me.

From *El NUEVO Piense Y Hágase Rico*...

> Los pensamientos que una persona coloca deliberadamente en su propia mente, y anima con simpatía, y con la combinación de una o varias de las emociones, ¡constituyen las fuerzas motivantes que dirigen y controlan cada uno de sus movimientos, acciónes, y logros!

Hey, what that is saying, and again, maybe you hear it another way this time, is,

> Thoughts which a person deliberately places in their own mind, and encourages with sympathy, and with which they mix any one or more of the emotions, constitute the motivating forces, which direct and control their every movement, act, and deed!

These thoughts which YOU plant constitute the motivating forces that drive and control every single action, movement, and success you have.

Surf www.ThinkRich.com * Quantum Business Acceleration, $197 value gift *FREE*

That's how deep you want to *plant* your definite chief aim, your greatest desires, your causes, your family, everything that you're working together with. Like it's destiny – because it is. Do it deliberately, with passion and intent, so you get the rewards that are possible to you.

SHEEPLE ACTUALLY BELIEVE THE GOVERNMENT IS GOING TO HELP THEM!

I get a kick out of some people, and sometimes I use a mildly pejorative term. (Maybe it should serve as a wakeup call). I call them "sheeple". These are folks who actually believe the government is going to help them, who actually believe the government is going to solve their problems.

Now, I'm not an iconoclast—I've got other issues to fight. I'm much more concerned about business growth and personal development. *But* let's take one example in modern America.

I'm a marketer who uses a lot of mail. And believe me, brother, it's a last resort to use the U.S. Postal Service. They're incompetent, they're ungrateful, they're as uninspiring as it comes… I hate to even go into the post office. You know about the long lines and waits.

But look to the competitors. These are businesses, not governments: FedEx, UPS, and DHL, for example. They're prompt, they're excited, they're courteous, they're efficient. What a difference!

I'm not saying there doesn't need to be government; there does. Someone has to build the infrastructure, someone has to perform the duties of the police; there has to be *some* government. But government business doesn't even count, because you've got the same government mentality.

They expect a free ride.

You know, there are millions and millions of Americans who are working for companies that can't afford to give them insurance—whereas the people who are slugs on the government payroll can't get fired! They can't…unless they do something just really outrageous. And they get great benefits. This is not efficiency, this is *in*efficiency.

So when the government enters or nationalizes a new business area, I cringe because they're *not* going to make it better; they're going to make it worse. I could go on and on, but I don't want you to get the wrong impression.

I'm not screaming "anti-government". To the contrary, I'm hollering "personal empowerment". You aren't a sheeple. You know the answer. Sheeple actually believe the government is going to *help* them!

INTENTION TRUMPS TIME

It's fairly well known in motivational circles and sporting circles... The story of Roger Bannister, the first person to break the four minute mile - or as they say it in the track and field arena, to run the *sub*-four minute mile.

What a lot of people don't know is what went on to make that happen. Let me just give you some insight—this guy *did* break a record they had been trying to break for thousands of years. You know the Olympics, they come from ancient Greece...speaking of which, he missed the 1948 Olympics.

But you see, he *was* a runner, and he *did* have talent, apparently. He was in school, young. And in fact, he did the error to himself—he just didn't believe he was up to the quality of it.

When he watched it on the black-and-white TV—I'm assuming that's how he heard about it, I don't know—he knew he had screwed up big time.

So he set in his sights the '52 Olympics, which he made. And in his two running events—he did a mile and, I think, he did 880 yards—he placed fifth in his prime event, the mile.

Now, it takes a lot to become an Olympic athlete, you've got to agree. We all know the stories and the practice and the discipline—you think?

Do you know most people don't know the guy was a very busy student at the very prestigious Oxford University??.. It's not like this was all he had to dedicate himself to...

It's not easy there, when you're studying pre-med neurosurgery—you know, the brain. They don't know he practiced a mere 30 minutes a day on his lunch hour. He had some intention there. He had some *focus* there.

They don't know after he placed fifth in the Olympics in 1952 he was crushed. That's fifth in the entire world, which *sounds* like some major, major cool thing...and it is. But if you're going for the Olympic gold, that's as failure as failure can come.

No lies. No hype. Fact.

They don't know he hurt on that, and they don't know it was at that moment he put his intention out - he put in his sights the sub-four minute mile.

They don't know he was preparing for that, training for that. Living that, eating that, breathing that. Laying to sleep and bouncing to feet with that... That *was* his goal. That it was his specific goal and crowning glory...

They don't know the day he did it he called it - he told his pacemaker, "The sub four minute attempt is on."

Now you know that. Now you know the importance of getting your game in order, and you know that it can be done in short, regular, focused, intense training, with intention. Now you see the incredible value of intention. Intention trumps time.

Intention trumps time, every time.

Put it to work for *your* activities.

TUNE INTO WHAT YOU WANT

Sintonize con lo que si quiere, nunca lo que no quiere.

We're saying tune in to and with what you *want*, not with what you *don't* want. This concept was well illustrated in *The Secret,* the movie by Rhonda Byrne. Remember the bills, the aggravation, people at the mailbox? And of course the message of the movie was, because you're thinking that way, that's what you keep getting. It's the law of attraction.

Quantum physics shows it works.

And well, lo and behold, the message is the same here. Tune into what you *want,* not what you *don't* want. Now here's a good one, though—what if you don't *have* what you want right now, how do you tune into that? Well, it's easy. You imagine it in vivid color and brightness, high-intensity sounds, sight, size... change the mental dimensions as NLP teaches you to do.

And you make it so valuable you will do anything to go for it. That you actually put yourself in motion, in action, with a definite plan to manifest it. *That's* how you do it. Tune into what you *want*. Amplify that want. You've got a life to live; you've got a chance to make something of it.

No guarantees. Time goes fast. What are you gonna do? It's up to you.

If you are conscious, if you're really wanting to create the kind of things a lot of people attracted to this philosophy are, it's real simple.

Again, the message comes up—connect yourself, tune in to the thing you *want*, not the things you *don't* want. Work the law of attraction the proper way: *for* you, not against you.

NOTES

Item / passage / page	Insight	Action

BUS OUTSIDE THE BOX

I want to talk about creative thinking and the ability to look outside the box, the ability to *visit* outside the box and see what actually may not even be considered creative thinking somewhere else—and *bam,* it's a breakthrough for you. And I'm going to use a simple little example.

Not too long ago, I needed to cross the continent in Panamá. You know, I normally would take a car, I normally would drive, I normally would go with someone...I mean, Jiminy Christmas, it's *only* 50 or 60 miles wide. That's how wide the continent is there...that's how long it takes to get from the south to the north in that country.

But, because I was going to Colón, to the north coast, to the Atlantic Coast, to *pick up* a vehicle I needed to bring back—well, driving wasn't a very good solution. And it was in the middle of a workday, so I didn't have too many people who could take me. Nobody takes a taxi for 50 miles.

So I just said, "Hey, I'll take the bus!" You know, the bus instead of a taxi. And my wife just rolled her eyes. She couldn't believe I would do such a thing. But I'm telling you, it was an air- conditioned bus, quiet, it was shaded, had curtains on the windows. There was ample room.

It was the perfect bus ride, and get this, it cost $2.50 to go 50 miles. *That* was a break-over/shake-over.

That's not the creative thinking I'm talking about. Here's what I'm talking about. I went to the Transporte Nacional in Albrook—in other words, I went to a transportation center—and I went through the thing thinking that I'm getting on this bus and we'll be leaving right away. "There's a bus here; we'll be leaving right away."

No, no...see, I'm used to the American, to the Hong Kongese, to the British systems of "efficiency and schedules". *Schedules,* you know.

Nooo—down there they just wait. That's exactly what they do; and when the bus fills up they leave. They don't *run* empty buses.

Now, that's got a good side and bad side. But I'm telling you, creative thinking... What if we tried that in a few American cities? Some of these buses I see running around, I'm saying, "These people can't be making money." They're being financed by some other aspect, maybe our tax dollars, right?

Creative thinking. You see, the bus doesn't leave when it's timed, the bus leaves when it's full. Now, I know that won't work in every situation, and on a lot of bus routes they have pickups and drop-offs all along the way instead of being just *here we go from here to there*. On this run, though there where stops on the Colón end, it all left from the central terminal.

But it doesn't hurt to understand, and to know about, and to practice *lateral thinking*. To think about how you can apply any novel idea you encounter in *one* field into another. And to travel and keep your eyes open... All these are very good things for an achiever.

THE CRAZY THING'S ENTIRELY POSSIBLE

I'm often asked about *the crazy thing's entirely possible*. I am asked about *HoloMagic*. Well, let me tell you this. It starts in the individual. We are a big vibratory universe. We are a big quantum soup. This is the world quantum physics reveals to us. Every single one of us is equally capable in this quantum soup. What we think about, we bring about.

What *we* think about we bring about—even if we're believing things that are erroneous, as in, "I can't do this." Or one thing that would apparently be erroneous, as some people have accused —"I *can* do this." Either way, the crazy thing's entirely possible.

Let me think just a little bit. Michael Dell—billions. Employs tens of thousands. He started in a garage. He did this in just a few short years.

Michael O' Hagan, who you may or may not know of—I know about him because I connect a little bit more with Australia than most Americans do—is a backpacker who arrived from New Zealand. New Zealanders are kind of thought of as second class there a little bit.

He went from the backpack to a multi-millionaire with a moving company based on a unique idea that's taken off all across Australia, not just where he started. It didn't just stay a little local business.

And now it's franchised, and I know for a *fact* he's talking to people in other countries. And I know for a *fact* he's been visiting in the U.S. with a couple of different interested parties.

Sergey Brin and Larry Page, a couple of college boys, figured out people would like to be able to search the web and get *relevant* results. That's what they basically figured out. Billionaires today.

Bill Bowerman and Phil Knight—you know, I bought a Nike product the other day. It was just a weight training belt, and the instructions that I got, just a pamphlet folded so many times, were written in *27 languages*. I read Spanish and English, and those were the same at least.

Bill Bowerman, a retired coach from the University of Oregon, and Phil Knight started that up. *Nothing, nothing.* Bill Bowerman made the first set of Nikes on his wife's waffle iron.

Bill Gates was just a kid too, and a college drop-out, by the way. He only took the courses that meant something to him—computer stuff. He took a gamble, took a risk, made an intelligent business decision. *Richest man* in the world.

Harlan Sanders had some setbacks at 62, which forced him into selling the only thing he had of value – a formula for good tasting chicken.

And Ray Kroc was a non-descript nobody – a route salesman for malt machines at 52. *Billions* served; billion$ made!

The crazy thing's entirely possible! We've been talking billions and billions. That's a lot a HoloMagic! And it all starts in the individual, with vision, faith, determination, and *action!*

I'M GOING TO BE AN AUTHOR!

I just got through reading an article I myself had written profiling Panamauro, the King of Trash, the man who had a realization at the age of six or seven, putting together an *incredible* combination of business sense. He decided that everybody had trash, always would, and that he liked trash.

He connected it together at that young age with business. He knew that we always generate trash, and he would always have money coming in forever if he got involved in trash. And fast forward—he's a *world leader* in trash. *Surprise! Surprise!*

And so, I took it from there... I said, "Ted, what have you done? Where are you at?" Because, remember the R2A2 formula: we always read, relate, assimilate and act. So how am I assimilating this, relating it to me?

I likewise had a realization early on that never changed that I have fulfilled.

It happened in the second grade, and I remember the *instant* that *I knew*. It's more appropriate to say I *knew* than it is to say I *decided*, although they may have both happened in the same moment, and it certainly had to do with my attractions and infatuations up to that point in life.

We're all—and this is Nature—at the point where we're thinking about the future at that age.

I was in the second grade, seven years old, Mrs. Matlock was the teacher. I always chose to sit near *the rear* of the class near one side, so accordingly, I was sitting in the left lower rear of the class. We had school desks for every individual student. They had a top that hinged up and underneath that top that hinged up, you had your school supplies.

My dad was in the civil service at the time, during the Cold War. This is when the computers were the size of a room instead of the size of a laptop. This was in the late '50's.

And I'm reaching into my desk, because my dad had all these reams of computer paper that I got to use for free that he brought home, recycling, mind you, because it was no longer of use to the government.

So, when I'm reaching in my desk, Mrs. Matlock is talking, and I pop up a piece of paper just like always, pop it up, and at the instant I began that motion, the energy goes through my whole corpus, through my whole body. "I'm going to be an author!" That is when and how the realization came.

What does a second grader say? "I'm going to be an author!"

No fireman, no surgeon, no restaurateur. "I'm going to be an author!" Now, that became a whole lot more than I thought it was. It really meant, "I'm going to be an entrepreneur." But it's easy to be an entrepreneur in pursuit of your definite chief aim to be an author.

It *happened*. It was *done!*

THEY'RE NOT IN MOTION ACCOMPLISHING THEIR OWN DREAMS

Truly, I wouldn't want the job if it was given to me, and they've got so much of this talk about creating new jobs. I'm going to talk about TSA, the Transportation Security Administration.

I'm in the airport and I see these people, like bees or ants—they just swarm over, and they've got all these useless agents and there are people sitting there *bored,* and there are people chit-chatting.

I think, "Man, at this time of economic crisis in the U.S., we're not creating jobs! We're *making* jobs." Which *is* the President's plan, but they're worthless pieces of *crap*! These people are not productive, they're not going anywhere in their life, and they think that they're getting benefits from the government.

Now, I know you would *never* be so foolish as to think you're getting a gift from your government. No, they always *take* more than they give. And that's the whole point of this thing: evaluate. Just because people are *swarming* to these jobs, it's because they don't have a higher vision. They're not in motion accomplishing their own dreams.

Let this be a warning to you, let this be a reminder to you, of the reasons why *you* have such a much more fulfilling life. One of them is that you're *doing* something, instead of just *sitting* there being bored, occasionally telling a person, "You can't go that way," or "If you go that way, you're going to have to go through security again."

You're not a person who is running those little tubs back and forth all day, thinking they're mighty, mighty important... Or even *worse* a supervisory person one level up, who *really* thinks they're mighty important.

Again, it's the old J. Paul Getty thing... Whose train are you on? Are you getting ahead? Or are you a moving train, going to their destination, not yours, and thinking you are making progress?

NOTES

Item / passage / page	Insight	Action

I Am Reminded Of The Shortness Of Life

I don't know why I am compelled by HoloCosm to bring up this topic of productivity again—specifically, recognizing that there's only a finite amount of space and time we as human beings have to be productive in, in a way that has leverage and compounding benefit.

Two people who, in some manner or another, I am or have been connected with, who were in perfectly good health, have died over the last couple of weeks. As I'm writing this, one died last night at 2 a.m.—that's why I'm mentioning this.

The first: Hal Jones, a very respected banker, was getting out of his car in the parking lot and going into his office—when a hired gun came up behind him and shot him twice through the back of his skull. Amazingly, he survived, somewhat, for two weeks in a coma.

This vibrant young man was just getting out of his car to go to work one normal, ordinary day when he was murdered. This man had business relationships, he was respected, he was head of two different banking associations at different times in the Bahamas, where he was working the last number of years. He's actually from North Wales, England, U.K.

And it's over.

Now, in the U.S. I live with some roommates—this is the current situation. In Panamá I live with my wife and daughter. So I have Latino roommates on both sides of the border, by the way. Well, I wake up with the bad news that the wife of one of my roommates' uncles has passed away.

It's now late in the day, and he's been sad all day. He's from a Latino country—he's been wearing a white rosary around his neck all day. It's a Sunday, so we happen to be here, around more.

Heart attack. Amelia. He even pulled out some video, remembering her, and I saw her less than 365 days ago. She was 49, 50 now, on the video; she was in perfectly good health. Nobody saw the heart attack coming, at 2 a.m. in the morning. It happened in her sleep.

I am reminded of the shortness of life. I am reminded of the uncertainty. I am reminded we don't have to go through a period of decline to our final day. I am reminded the *only thing* we have is the present, not the future.

We have the future to create, and we do need to be productive, insofar as what we do today does connect tomorrow for the next five, 10, 20, 30, 50, 60, 2,000 years. But we ourselves won't be around for it. We can only live today, we create today. We can't put off living any longer.

Seize the day, *carpe* diem, *contribute*!

FIND YOUR ETERNITY IN EACH MOMENT

"You must live in the present. Launch yourself on every wave. Find your eternity in each moment." Henry David Thoreau said that. Here we are, talking about eternity. Here we are, describing HoloMagic. Henry David Thoreau, the transcendentalist, said it in the 1800's. He said a lot of other important things, too, like, "The mass of men lead lives of quiet desperation."

Those are the two alternatives.

The mass of men—he would have said *people* today—lead lives of quiet desperation. Then he says to us: "You must live in the present. Launch yourself on every wave. Find your eternity in each moment." That's a big difference between quiet desperation and living with passion.

And that's the position of creative, actualizing individuals who *decide* what they want to contribute to this *Earth*, their contribution for having the chance to pass this way. Further, *knowing that the law* works—they go after it in the *way* they choose.

Surely, surely, if you use good marketing, everything is selling. It's getting into your zone. A lot of the times that's getting outside your *comfort* zone.

You see, when you're doing something new, when you're reaching for a new thing, when it's a time of change, whether circumstances come upon you, or whether you have a desire to go after more, *you can stir the fire and passion within*.

We have events to help you do just that. That's one of the things the firewalk is all about. With focus and intention, boom, you can do it.

That's the entire purpose behind neural repatterning.

But the difference between your life and *lives of quiet desperation*, the lives a lot of your friends, neighbors, media, and people on the street are leading, is that you must *live* in the present. They call it a "present". Be creative. "Launch yourself on every wave. Find your eternity in each moment."

NOTES

Item / passage / page	Insight	Action

WITHOUT HEALTH YOU DON'T HAVE ANYTHING

I recorded the audio for this article while I was at Tocumen International Airport, Panamá City, Panamá, heading back to the U.S. for a little visit there. Boy, I'll tell you what—it takes a little getting used to, having this face mask I've been wearing. But I do believe it's a good *investment*.

I've always thought a lot about politicians. I guess I'm just like everybody else—I have a love/hate relationship with them, you know. They know much more than you, and they have more contacts and they're spending your money, and they want more of your money—and on and on and on. But they *definitely* are the rulers of the country.

I mean, when the *Vice President of the United States of America* says he would not advise *any* of his family members, any people he loves, to travel on a plane—well, brother, sister, he knows something you and I don't know. He *knows* more than you and I know. I'll take it to heart. I'll take it to heart in a heartbeat.

The *swine flu* could be another plague. I'm going to do my part to put it off. Hey, let's talk about it for a moment. What is achievement? What is the ability to contribute? Hey, it's doing what you've got to do, whatever it takes.

And right now, it takes guarding your health in a way that you might not have done it before. Not everybody's that hep to it. I know here in the airport, they've issued the masks to *all* the employees. Apparently there is no enforcement, because it looks like only about fifteen percent are wearing them. I'd advise you to.

You can get a mask easily. You might be able to get one at a medical supply house... I couldn't. Man, *they were all sold out*. One of the schools was having a get-together, and everybody was buying them. You can also get them at Lowe's or Home Depot. That'll work for you.

Taking care of yourself, doing whatever it takes, guarding your health, we often talk about that in the context of this philosophy.- because without health, you don't have anything. It *could* happen to you. It *could*. I'll give you a little anecdote about how close it could get.

Yeah. Hey, who knows? I myself, as well as you yourself, may already have it and don't even know it.

I took my little seven-year-old daughter to school this morning, before coming here to the airport to take the afternoon flight, and golly gee, about an hour later, she's coming back home. School's closed for a *week*. *Someone* in the school has been detected with *swine flu*. Of course, they changed the name to H1N1 to keep other imbecile governments from slaughtering all the swine in their country in a hasty over-reaction. It was poorly named, when it had nothing to do with swine.

My little sweetheart, she can say it right off. I don't pay that much attention to it. I just know that I need to be aware of it and take protective measures. So here's the interesting thing, though—she was in the school, and it came. It *may* already be *in my house*. I mean, it doesn't *always* happen to *other* Georges. It happens to *all* of us.

Guard your health. You don't know. I encourage you.

By the way, I actually think I look good in this mask. It's the first time I've played doctor in my life! How about you? Anyway, we can have a sense of humor about what's happening.

Do what you can, friend. I love you. I want you to stay here for a long time.

Index

"You Are Closer To A Million Dollar$ Than You Now Dream!"

This is the modernized, quantum empowered version of Napoleon Hill's success classic , *Think And Grow Rich!*

#1 Best-Seller

An instruction manual to *consciously* direct the Quantum universe to manifest your positive desires."

Napoleon Hill Overlooks Ted Ciuba
Physical, Kindle. iStore

Are you ready for breakthrough progress overnight?!

Engage with *The New Think And Grow Rich* - empower yourself! Start exactly where you are - no experience, no education, no cash required! Discover how to…

- Trigger the *self-fulfilling prophecy* and the *law of attraction*!
- Apply the insights of the secret "combination" to work for your immediate, easy success
- Direct the Quantum universe to deliver success
- Unleash that powerful "HoloMagic c2 factor" to accomplish your pursuits in a fraction of the time, with only a quanta of the effort to reap HUGE, AMAZING, WINDFALL results!

Mark Whyborn, UK

*"I have read **The New Think And Grow Rich** and there is a **HUGE improvement** (so much more insight) in the new updated version!*

Once you learn the formula to riches, you can apply it to accelerate your income into the stratosphere!

Order now, for you and your company & loved ones. Available at http://www.amazon.com, www.BarnesAndNoble.com, & any reputable bookstore.

www.ThinkRich.com/book

"Now You Can Effortlessly Transmute Commuting Down-Time To Financial Independence!"

Not Available Anywhere Else!!

Announcing!

The NEW Think and Grow Rich In Audio

Rare Footage!

Word-for-word reading by the author, so you understand *every* word just as it was intended!

Ted Ciuba expresses, emotes, renders, and interprets word-for-word the simple but deceptively complex information contained in the **13 named principles of *The NEW Think And Grow Rich - secrets** behind every millionaire's success</u> - none of which requires a thin dime.

Napoleon Hill First Discovered The Secret - Ted Ciuba Took It To New Heights In A New Age!

- Catch the true meaning and significance
- Tune into the emotions, vocal inflections, and all the other dimensions that give the *spoken* word superior communication ability over the written word!

The easiest way to fast-track your success!

Take *The NEW Think and Grow Rich*
At the "University on Wheels" - your car or transport!

www.TheNewThinkAndGrowRichAudio.com

It has a record setting history!

"Short, regular, focused, intense, intended training sessions could mean riches and fulfillment to *you!*"

Most intelligent people agree that to get ahead, you must go the extra mile. But the amazing thing is, it takes *so little* to excel!

**After all, it's called the extra *mile*,
not the extra *100 miles!***

Apart From Massive Intention, It Didn't Take Much

Roger Bannister
Runs sub 4 Minute Mile

Roger Bannister defied and redefined history by running the sub 4 minute mile. Exact time: 03:59.4/10's. 6 May 1954, Roger Bannister redefined human possibility by clocking in a mere 6/10's of a *second* sub 4 minutes.
And the amazing thing is that Bannister did NOT spend countless hours training... He gave it what he could in his busy pre-med schedule... A mere 30 minutes a day!!

And with that he set broke a barrier that had stood 3,000 years!

Then, within 2 1/2 years of Bannister's unachievable, record-breaking sub 4 minute mile, 18 others were doing it.

 It's Your Turn! And now you can run the extra mile by tuning into a sub 4 minute length daily audio or video message with incredible motivation, insights, and training in a wide variety of fields always centered around the philosophy of *The NEW Think And Grow Rich*.

The compounding of simply sub 4 minutes every day is incredible!

You, too, can defy the status quo in **short, regular, focused, intense, intended training sessions** and **redefine what's possible for you!**

It takes so little to excel. Visit the website and get started today:

www.BigBriefMoments.com

"How Quickly Would Your Life Improve If You Began Using The Untapped 90% Of Your Brain To Bring You Wealth?!"

Revolutionary new neuroscience driven

HoloMagic Wealth Programming
Installs *The NEW Think and Grow Rich* Philosophy In You Effortlessly!

Amazing new neurosynergist® technology vaults leagues beyond ordinary hypnosis to effectuate immediate and permanent changes in your inner "wealth tracks"!

HoloMagic Wealth Programming

"Strap on your headphones, change your world!"

HoloMagic Wealth Programming is the *only* neural repatterning system in the world based on the proven principles of *The NEW Think And Grow Rich* using the patented neurosynergist® sound technology.

Dives to the depths of your *delta* subconscious, at the level where you connect with HoloCosm, and reprograms you to have and express the attitudes, strategies, and action-taking skills of the super wealthy.

Advanced thinkers, human potential experts, and the quantum and neuroscience labs affirm that the world you live in is a reflection of your inner world – the thoughts you consistently hold in your mind.

- Unleash the 90% realm of the brain that few people access and find your fortunes using the principles of *The NEW Think and Grow Rich!*…
- Put this cutting-edge, powerful, neural repatterning system to work for you!
- Visit:

www.WealthProgramming.com

"Discover The "Secret" In A Magical Mastermind Study Of The 1937 *Original Publication* Of Napoleon Hill's Success Classic, *Think And Grow Rich*!"

Achiever's MasterMind

You actively participate in working study sessions... DESIGNED WITH THE SOLE PURPOSE OF MAKING YOU WEALTHY!

www.AchieversMasterMind.com

Includes:

1. Sixteen Achiever's MasterMind Sessions In Audio
2. Achiever's MasterMind Study Chapters
1. *Achiever's MasterMind* Study Guides

Bonuses include word-for-word transcriptions!

- How to do direct imprinting into your nervous system, so that you're driven to success!
- How to harness the awesome unseen power that has created Fortunes with one secret 6-step technique. (Takes less than 5 minutes to implement.)
- The 8-part, no-fail secret the winners in the wealth game use to... Create your own "breaks"
- And much, much more!

Digital Version – Save $$$! – Audio and print files downloadable instantly!

Physical Version - so you can feed CD's into your CD player and carry the convenient notebooks with you!

www.AchieversMasterMind.com

East-West Success MasterMind
Merging The Success Secrets Of Two Worlds

"If You're Looking For That Decided Edge That Can Accelerate You To Riches!..."

Author of *The NEW Think And Grow Rich*, Ted Ciuba, journeyed East to forge this collaboration. The entire event was captured, and is available to you now as the...

East-West Success MasterMind
www.EastWestSuccessMasterMind.com

Share the excitement that got people tuning in from Singapore, Malaysia, China, Hong Kong, Vietnam, Korea, Philippines, Thailand, India, Australia, UK, USA, Africa, and Latin America!

The purpose of the MasterMind is quite simple...

In a MasterMind study of the success philosophy outlined in the original *Think And Grow Rich*...

- To merge the BEST of both East and West to enable any willing human being, anywhere on this planet *or any other planet or moon*, to THINK WITH INTENT...
- To control and direct your thinking to receive the *natural result* of RICHES in your life!

"One of the most important days of my life was the day I began to read Think and Grow Rich." - W. Clement Stone

"I was invited to participate in the MasterMind *study of* Think And Grow Rich *by my friend Ted Ciuba. That 8-week program transformed my own Consciousness of Wealth...* - Dan Klatt

www.EastWestSuccessMasterMind.com

Who Else Would Like To Have

The NEW Think and Grow Rich Author Ted Ciuba Motivate and Train Your Group?

Schedule permitting, Ted Ciuba welcomes keynote, speaking and training invitations from businesses, organizations, associations, and promoters.

The quantum performance message of *The New Think And Grow Rich* and *Sub 4 Minute Extra Mile* is perfectly suited to anyone in pursuit of money, a career, sales, and a life!

Through a brief but thorough pre-event questionnaire, Ted Ciuba makes each presentation unique to each group.

To discuss opportunities and arrangements contact our organization by email at events@holomagic.com or from the website at www.ThinkRich.com

Ted Ciuba On Stage In LA

Additional Copies Of
The NEW Think And Grow Rich
At A Discount

This book reveals the key to unlocking your wealth, the secret formula to riches, the combination to the vault of abundance in modern terms and in modern ways.

Individuals have bought this book, looking to forge their destiny of riches. They've in turn, bought this book for their friends and family members, hoping to impart the mystical magic of its power. Suggested it to their employers, to distribute the book and train on it.

Entrepreneurs and coaches buy this book for their team members. Insurance and real estate companies buy this book for all the personnel in their organizations. Multi-level companies and all sales forces make this book required reading - to achieve outstanding success at any age. Motivators and business opportunities experts demand you read this book.

Companies have even bought this book and *given* it to their *customers*! Talk about an enlightened company!

To get a discount on multiple copies visit…

www.HoloMagic.com/ntr/multiple.html